T0089728

Tropic of Squalor

Tropic of Squalor

Poems

MARY KARR

HARPER PERENNIAL

NEW YORK • LONDON • TORONTO • SYDNEY • NEW DELHI • AUCKLAND

HARPER ● PERENNIAL

FIRST HARPER PERENNIAL EDITION PUBLISHED 2020.

Library of Congress Cataloging-in-Publication Data has been applied for.

ISBN 978-0-06-269983-1 (pbk.)

20 21 22 23 24 LSC 10 9 8 7 6 5 4 3 2 1

For Dev & Sarah every dang day,
for Don DeLillo & Philip Roth on holy days,
    & (wincingly enough) for Jesus:
you all keep me kneeling down and looking up

Acknowledgments

Ever grateful for my editrix, Jennifer Barth at HarperCollins, who keeps pages rolling out. Ditto for readers like Rodney Crowell, Betty Sue Flowers, Sarah Harwell, Brooks Haxton, Terrance Hayes, Amy Koppelman, Herb Leibowitz, Paul Muldoon, Sarah Paley, and George Saunders.

Thanks also to the following publishers:

The New Yorker: "The Organ Donor's License Has a Black Check," "Illiterate Progenitor," "Recuperation from the Dead Love Through Christ and Isaac Babel" (published here as "Petering: Recuperation from the Sunk Love Under the Aegis of Christ and Isaac Babel"), "Face Down," "Carnegie Hall Rush Seats."

Poetry: "Loony Bin Basketball," "The Burning Girl," "Read These," "Suicide's Note: An Annual," "The Obscenity Prayer," "Awe and Disorder," "The Blessed Mother Complains to the Lord Her God about the Abundance of Brokenness She Receives," "A Perfect Mess."

Parnassus: "Animal Planet," "Bolt Action," "The Age of Criticism."

Commonweal: "The Voice of God," "The Devil's Delusion," "Messenger."

Ploughshares: "Psalm for Riding a Plane" (published here as "Notes from the Underground").

Carl Jung carved this Latin inscription above the door to his Swiss house: *Vocatus atque non vocatus deus aderit.* "Summoned or not summoned, the god will be there."

Contents

Tropic of Squalor

The Organ Donor's Driver's License
Has a Black Check

Forgive me, black ant at the base of my yoga mat:
if the Buddhists are right, and you had a soul,
I'm a killer. And you, young buck whose suede neck

through the rifle's scope I might otherwise
have stroked. Forgive me juicy burger medium rare.
I fell off the vegan wagon for want of you.

I devoured your iron to fuel my weak blood.
Jet-lagged from the Paris flight, I slumped
and felt your sacrifice worthy. How'd you go?

A bolt through the skull and your big corpus
on the blood-gelled floor of the abattoir.
Countless ducks flying their arrowheads

across the gray sky found their emerald necks
in my bird dog's mouth. I liked what Dean said
to the squirrel we found thrashing on the path

off the quad. He'd stopped to look down—
his lips blue from his failing heart as if he had eaten
nothing but Bomb Pops for a week. Some beast

must have crunched down on the squirrel's neck,
and Dean bent like a waiter to say (sans
irony) *I honor your struggle, little brother.*

Loony Bin Basketball

(for Phil Jackson)

The gym opened out
before us like a vast arena, the bleached floorboards
yawned toward a vanishing point, staggered seats high
as the Mayan temple I once saw devoured by vines.
Each of us was eaten up inside — all citizens of lost
    and unmapped cities.

Frank hugged the pimply ball
over his belly like an unborn child. Claire
dressed for day care in daffodil yellow and jelly shoes.
David's gaze was an emperor's surveying a desiccated
battlefield. Since he viewed everything that way, we all
    saw him the same.

The psych techs in cloroxed white
were giant angels who set us running drills, at which
we sucked. The zones we set out to defend were watery
at every edge. We missed close chest passes, easy combos.
Our metronomes run different tempos,
    John proclaimed.

Then Claire started seeing
dashes stutter through the air behind the ball.
Then speed lines on our backs, and then her own head
went wobbly as a spinning egg. She'd once tracked
planetary orbits for NASA and now sat sidelined
    by her eyes' projections.

Only Bill had game.
Catatonic Bill whose normal talent was to schlub
days in a tub chair — his pudding face scarred
with chicken pox — using his hand for an ashtray,
belly for an armrest. Now all that peeled away, and he
    emerged, clean as an egg.

He was a lithe
and licorice boy, eeling past all comers, each shot
sheer net. He faked both ways, went left. Beneath the orange
rim his midair pirouettes defied the gravity that I
could barely sludge through. He scored beyond what even
    Claire could count,

then he bent panting,
hands on knees as the orderlies held out water cups,
and the rest of us reached to pat his back or slap
his sweaty hand, no one minding about the stench or his
breath like old pennies. Then as quick as that
   he went.

Inside his head
some inner winch did reel him back from the front
of his face bones where he'd been ablaze. He went back and
back into that shadowed stare. Lucky we were to breathe
his air. Breath is God's intent to keep us living. He was
   the self I'd come in

wanting to kill, and I left him there.

The Burning Girl

While the tennis ball went back and forth in time
    A girl was burning. While the tonic took its greeny
        Acid lime, a girl was burning. While the ruby sun fell
From a cloud's bent claws and Wimbledon was won
    And lost, we sprawled along the shore in chairs,
        We breathed the azure air alongside
A girl with the thinnest arms all scarred and scored
    With marks she'd made herself—
        She sat with us in flames
That not all saw or saw but couldn't say at risk
    Of seeming impolite. And later we all thought
        Of the monk who'd doused himself with gas,
Lit a match, then sat unmoving and alert amid
    Devouring light. She didn't speak. She touched
        No aspect of our silly selves.
We were a herd of hardly troubled rich.
    She was an almost ghost her mother saw
        Erasing the edges of herself each day

Smudging the lines like charcoal while her parents
    Redrew her secretly into being over and
        Again each night and dawn and sleepless
All years long. Having seen that mother's love,
    I testify: It was ocean endless. One drop could've
        Brought to life the deadest Christ, and she
Emptied herself into that blazing child with all her might
    And stared a hundred million miles into
        The girl's slender, dwindling shape.
Her father was the devoted king of helicopter pad
    And putting green. His baby burned as we
        All watched in disbelief.
I was the facile friend insisting on a hug
    Who hadn't been along for years of doctors, wards,
        And protocols. I forced her sadness close. I said
C'mon let's hug it out. Her arms were white
    Birch twigs that scissored stiffly at my neck till she
        Slid on. That night we watched
Some fireworks on the dewy lawn for it was
    Independence Day. By morning she was gone.
        She was the flaming tower we all dared

To jump from. So she burned.

Illiterate Progenitor

My father lived so far from the page,
  the only mail he got was marked OCCUPANT.
    The century had cored him with its war, and he paid
      bills in person, believed in flesh and the family plan.

In that house of bookish females, his glasses slid on
  for fishing lures and carburetor work,
    the obits, my report cards, the scores.
      He was otherwise undiluted by the written word.

At a card table, his tales could entrance a ring of guys
  till each Timex paused against each pulse,
    and they'd stare like schoolboys even as he wiped
      from the center the green bills anted up.

Come home. I'm lonely, he wrote in undulating script.
  I'd left to scale some library's marble steps like Everest
    till I was dead to the wordlessness
      he was mired in, which drink made permanent.

He took his smoke unfiltered, milk unskimmed.
He liked his steaks marbled, fatback on mustard greens,
onions eaten like apples, split turnips dipped
into rock salt, hot pepper vinegar on black beans.

Read These

(for DFW)

The King did say
and his arm swept the landscape's foliage into bloom
where he hath inscribed the secret mysteries of his love
before at last taking himself away. His head away. His
recording hand. So his worshipful subjects must imagine
themselves in his loving fulfillment, who were no more
than instruments of his creation. Pawns.
Apparati. Away, he took himself and left us
studying the smudged sky. Soft pencil lead.

Once he was not a king, only a pale boy staring down
from the high dive. The contest was seriousness
he decided, who shaped himself for genus genius
and nothing less. Among genii, whoever dies first wins.
Or so he thought. He wanted the web browsers to ping
his name in literary mention nonstop on the world wide web.

He wanted relief from his head, which acted as spider
and inner web weaver. The boy was a live thing tumbled in
its thread and tapped and fed off, siphoned from. His head
kecked back and howling from inside the bone castle from
    whence he came
to hate the court he held.

His loneliness was an invisible crown
rounding his brow tighter than any turban,
more binding than a wedding band,
and he sat becircled by his tower
on the rounding earth.

                                        Read these,
did say the King, and put down his pen, hearing
himself inwardly holding forth on the dullest
aspects of the tax code
with the sharpest possible wit. Unreadable
as Pound on usury or Aquinas on sex.

I know the noose made an oval portrait frame for his face.
And duct tape around the base of the Ziploc
bag was an air-tight chamber
for the regal head—most serious relic,
breathlessly lecturing in the hall of silence.

Discomfort Food for the Unwhole

To check out, we line up our carts,
Each head bent over a shining phone.
Through these squares of light, we tap

Tap with opposable thumbs, and though each
Human unit occupies a small space, a few
Floor tiles, each believes that through the glow

In her hands she can reach far, so from-this-place
Far. Our sprawling alphabets include hearts
Or dollar signs or cartoon thumbs turned up or down

To vote some Barabbas alive or dead. But ours
Is a city of I-beams and mirrored towers.
Behind us stretch rows of iced Gulf shrimp, New

Zealand lamb, the Russian sturgeon's glistening
Black eggs, dewy orchids misty from Brazil—
So much from so many for so few and at such

Spectacular cost, and yet we cannot lift our heads
From our hands to look around. We cannot stop
Ourselves—each face hung forward off the neck

Of the corpse each self devours.

The Devil's Delusion

I lie on my back in the lawnchair to study
the trees claw up toward Heaven
They have all the sap I lack

It's doubt I send rivering cloudways
in great boiling torrents as if all creation
were a bad stage set I could wave way away

then I could cast my dark spells in a blink
and a flaming fingersnap—and
a universe de Mare pops up

so I win the everlasting argument against all
that was or will be or tiredly is
As if my soul would not in that blink

be obliterate   As if as the kids say

Dear Oklahoma Teen Smashed
on Reservation Road

Dean's heart had been long years stiffening in its cage,
    and he wheeled around a contraption
like a bumpy vacuum cleaner or rolling luggage
    with shunts from the box to his chest
into the very meat of him, and through a clear plastic circle
    strapped to his solar plexus,
Dean's hot blood went round and round in stutter step.
    I held it once to warm my hands.
With each artificial throb, I composed an ode,
    not for Dean's death, but for the boy
who lived reckless enough to die and plant a part
    in the gasping poet's flesh. Next,
Dean phoned from the squeaking gurney
    being rolled toward the blue
antiseptic light, the gods in green masks. Take
    care of Laurie, he said. I said,
Don't be a dick, this is not *Terms of Endearment*,
    and you're not Debra Winger.

Then click, he entered the ether. I lay in my house
    hearing ice cubes avalanche down
the fridge chute and every clock whisper and his wife's
    phone powered off. The boy was shocked
into sinus rhythm and beats on in Dean's otherwise
    scooped-out chest: Israel is built on bones.

The Age of Criticism

Franz calls to say my new book is quote
the worst thing he's ever read close quote.
His hollering makes my plastic earpiece quiver.
It's not that bad, I claim. But have I compared it
with the great prose works (Tolstoy, etcet.). Sure,
I said, it sucks—at which he slams the receiver down.

The message Franz once left
most everybody we knew—*Your envy of my work
must be terrible for you*—his ex-girlfriend actually got printed
on a tee shirt. He'd left her for a rich, adoring student
that fall, and on New Year's, Franz insulted Tom's wife,
so Tom chased him around a table laden with Triscuits

and jug wines of the most sordid variety, till tall,
barrel-chested Askald stopped Tom, palm
to flannel-shirt chest, to say—with a drunk's
well-chewed precision—*You're wrecking my high*.
Tom then lunged out into the snow to walk it off.
People started again stabbing cheese cubes

with red and green toothpicks, and somebody's blowsy wife
who'd cornered the Nobel laureate went back
to twirling a lock of just-then-graying hair
over his forehead, while in the bedroom,
her husband snored on a mattress sprawled
with pea coats and thrift-store furs. Tom

was supposed to die, but didn't; Deborah wasn't,
but did. Candlelit and slim in oxblood riding boots,
she wore a near see-through black silk blouse
with loose coils of red hair tumbling down the back.
She was about to dump the two smart guys who'd left
their wives for her. Hearing her quote Baudelaire that night,

I believed there might be no one more alluring alive.
But she killed herself. Last April, widowed at sixty,
she jumped off the high stadium of some snotty college
where she taught, and whether she died from grief
or scorn for self or someone gone, it still seems dumb.
Even Askald's sober now. And nobody invited Franz

anywhere for years before cancer took him,
though we often emailed each other his crisp,
venomous posts to reviewers. Everybody
claimed to forgive Franz because his father
bailed and his stepdad beat him. And critics
hoping to stave off one of his nasty, articulate

rants persisted on calling him a genius because, hey,
what if he was? But we all thought him an asshole,
which makes us assholes too. That's how criticism works.
Sit in a room voting this word or that onto
or off the page, you become a beauty cop,
a scold, charged to carry that appraising gaze

to the faces of those you were sent to love.
I once sat with Franz in the day room
of his first loony bin near Christmas—
his face swollen from drink, his glasses
broken so a Band-Aid taped one wing on.
We smoked near a piano where a stick man

with wobbly eye pencil and graying hair
like mine now played *Someone to Watch Over Me*
while we wondered who might be dumb enough
to print our books or read them or
give us jobs, which happened, which failed
to soothe us more than sitting on that orange

plastic couch in shared dread. Lights blinking.
The ward nurse saying the boxes under the tree
were decorative only: they sat unopened every year.
Look at us passing my last smoke back and forth,
unable to guess we'd ever be anywhere
else, thick snow coming down and piling up,

sawhorses blocking all the small roads.

Exurbia

In the predawn murk when the porch lights hang
on suburban porches like soft lemons
my love rides out in his black car.

His high beams stroke our bedroom wall.
Half awake, I feel watched over and doze
afloat in swirls of white linen.

Then he's at the Y in trunks I bought him
sleek as an otter, eyes open behind goggles.
He claws the length of his lane.

Oh but his flip turn makes of his body
a spear, and his good heart drubs.
We often call at odd hours from different

star points of the globe. But today
he'll stop home to deposit a hot coffee
on my bedside. For years I fought

moving to this rich gulag because I thought
it was too white or too right or too dumb, but
really, as Blake once said,

I couldn't bear the beams of love.

Lord, I Was Faithless

I murdered you early, Father
My disbelief was an ice pick plunged
In mine own third eye

Like damned Oedipus
Whose sight could not stand
What his hand had done

And I—whose chief grumble
Was my kidhood (whose torments
Did fill many profitable volumes)

Refused your pedigree
I revised myself into a bastard
Orphan rather than serve

Like a poppet at your caprice
One among many numbered
To live size extra small

Whole years I lost in the kingdom
Of mine own skull
With my scepter the remote

I sat enthroned in a La-Z-Boy
Watching dramas I controlled
Only the volume on

I was a poor death's head then
In my hook-rug empire
With snowflakes of paper

My favorite button is power

Suicide's Note: An Annual

I hope you've been taken up by Jesus
though so many decades have passed, so far apart we'd grown
    between love transmogrifying into hate and those sad letters
        and phone calls and your face vanishing into a noose
that I couldn't
    today name the gods
        you at the end worshiped, if any, praise being
impossible for the devoutly miserable. And screw my Church who'd
    roast in Hell poor suffering
        bastards like you, unable to bear the masks
of their own faces. With words you sought to shape
    a world alternate to the one that dared
        inscribe itself so ruthlessly across your eyes, for you
could not, could never
    fully refute the actual or justify the sad heft of your body, earn
        your rightful space or pay for the parcels of oxygen
you inherited. More than once you asked
    that I breathe into your lungs like the soprano in the opera
    I loved so my ghost might inhabit you and you ingest

my belief in your otherwise-only-probable soul. I wonder does your
    death feel like failure to everybody who ever
        loved you as if our collective CPR stopped
too soon, the defib paddles lost charge, the corpse
    punished us by never sitting up. And forgive my conviction
        that every suicide's an asshole. There is a good reason
I am not God, for I would cruelly smite the self-smitten.
    I just wanted to say ha-ha, despite
        your best efforts you are every second
alive in a hard-gnawing way for all who breathed you deeply in,
    each set of lungs, those rosy implanted wings, pink balloons.
        We sigh you out into air and watch you rise like rain.

The Awakening
(after Milosz)

After decades of suffering the torments
Of mine own mind, I awoke one dawn
Breathing into the odd center of this
Once-orphaned flesh. Alive, blinking.
The edges of self neatly conscribed
By skin as by a cop's chalk outline.
My eyes rested on the actual surface
Of things. Nothing beamed from
My brain outward through the black
And spiral pinholes of mine eyes.
Nothing in me winced. This baffling
Stillness found me strapped in
The belly of a plane nosing west
Through blue air. I pinched my wristwatch
By its golden stem and pulled it out
And unwound its hands to undo
Whole hours, I could not not
Occupy my seat, could not wander

From the column of breath running up
The middle of me like rich sap of pine.
That inward root of air had ferried
The spirit of the Great Sustainer in
And out of nothingness all my miserable
Days and only in that instant did I feel
I *am* it. Wanting nothing, I failed
To fail at not having. How long
Did this stillness hold? The flesh went on
Ignorantly decaying. Then some baby's open
Drooling face popped above the forward seat
And I grasped in pity at it, which dropped me
In familiar agony again with want
That sweet black ribbon around mine throat.

How God Speaks

Not with face slap or body slam
Rarely with lightning bolt or thunderclap

But in sighs and inclinations leanings
The way a baby suckles breath

The green current of the hazel wand
Curves toward the underground spring

The man in cashmere flesh does arrive
Holding out his arms he is wide

As any horizon I've ever traversed desert for
He brings thread count to my bed

Fire to my oven   With a towel tucked
In his jeans he soaps my hair

Then finger combs it dry
I massage a knot from his neck

His mouth is well water
His gaze true and from

His tongue he brings the blessed Word

Face Down

What are you doing on this side of the dark?
You chose that side, and those you left
feel your image across their sleeping lids
as a blinding atomic blast.
Last we knew,
you were suspended midair
like an angel for a pageant off the room
where your wife slept. She had
to cut you down who'd been (I heard)
so long holding you up. We all tried to,
faced with your need, which we somehow
understood and felt for and took
into our veins like smack. And you
must be lured by that old pain smoldering
like wood smoke across the death boundary.
Prowl here, I guess, if you have to bother somebody.
Or, better yet, go bother God, who shaped
that form you despised from common clay.

That light you swam so hard away from
still burns, like a star over a desert or atop
a tree in a living room where a son's photos
have been laid face down for the holiday.

The Child Abuse Tour

We traveled into the lost time
    up the undulating hills
pine forests red clay earth
    I smelled being born
in streaming wood smoke
    the hairpin turns
the hard truth of dirt yards
    raked clean of any
grass blade swept watched over
    by bird dogs brindled
and ghost gray and copper
    alert to every leaf flicker
Then Cousin Peggy stood over
    the wooden bowl
her lean fencepost frame
    a repository of cruel
leukemia and a bone echo
    of Aunt Gladys
whose battered tin sifter did transform
    common cake flour into dust

powder finer than cocaine the sheen
    the rasp of the stiff hinge forcing
through the sifter's screen pale and
    paler moonlight into smaller
particles the wooden bowl came from
    Tennessee some seven
generations back tied in a croaker sack
    to an ox's ass bouncing   We knew
Peggy was dying and had journeyed out
    of our metropoli across desert
and frosted tundra a fur piece to watch
    her dead mother's hands
pinch the dumplings into chicken
    broth molten gold

The Less Holy Bible

Jesus said, "If you bring forth what is within you,
what you bring forth will save you.
If you do not bring forth what is within you,
what you do not bring forth will destroy you."
—Elaine Pagels, *The Gnostic Gospels*

I. Genesis: Animal Planet

I rose up first in a big vacant state with an x in its middle
to mark the place I was born into dying
surrounded by oil refinery towers with flames
like giant birthday candles you could never
get big enough to blow out. Before I was
they were, and before them, reptiles and mammals
died and rotted and were crushed into carbon
then coal, then oil in the earth
whose deep core held bigger burning.

My daddy labored here, at The Gulf,
Which meant *oil refinery*, but also
a distance he drowned in,
caged inside this high hurricane fence.
In steel-toed boots for forty-two years, he walked.
The gold hatpin he got at retirement
had four diamond chips
for a smile and two rubies like eyes,
and he passed it to me
because it was a holy relic

of suffering and sacrifice,
so I wanted it most.
He breathed in this chemical stink
some days sixteen hours or days on end
in a storm, and it perfumed his overalls.

The catalyst he pumped on the cracking unit
burst through with enormous pressure to break down
the black crude's chemical bonds
into layers, into products,
and many ignorant men did twist the spigots
and unplug the clogs and keep it all
rivering so the buried pipes
could carry out so many flammables north—

North! Where books are written and read.
The sunset down here glows green and hard-washed
denim blue and the scalded pink of flesh.

II. Numbers:
Poison Profundis

Row out in the bayou with a shovel.
Take a pistol case you cross a snake.
Some places they've dumped stuff.
   Sink a shovel in mud a few inches
   and comes seeping up
   some liquid stench right out
   of the earth bubbling
   acid green . . . like they took needles
   or serpent's fangs and injected
   the very ground with it.
   They dumped it here off trucks
   or buried it deep in barrels the stuff ate through.

The devil has his own cauldron
   and this goop glows green as any girl's
   magic clay she keeps on her nightstand.

We live on a scab, that's what I'm saying.
How much is that worth? Not spit, not the blood of those
boys dead now my brothers so young, Lord, wing them
away from this shithole.

III. Leviticus:
In Dreams Begin Responsibilities

No one had to announce it was deadly
more than a moccasin bite.

The dumbest guy here (picked from stiff competition)
knew he'd be extinguished soon, polluted.

The oil barons too smart to live here would
as soon snuff us out as look at us—

our spongy tumors, the scarlet growth
on the bird dog's belly, the fistula

in the breast, the bowels, the hanging balls,
basal cell carcinoma burned off with a cigarette.

Three gas stations in this town now chemo centers so
you needn't drive to Houston

to sit with pollution needled into your arm,
while far-off bosses who knew all along

hit pocked balls off small hickory tees
towards named greens that go forever on.

IV. Exodus: Bolt Action

I left home to escape the swamp of self.
The locusts swarmed as in the days of Job.
Each wore a prophet's face.

My mind was a charnel house and a death camp
and a mud pack body wrap in which you twist and steam
as every toxin leaches from your pores.

In every room of my home, the candles had been pinched dark,
the pages of the books wiped white of any word, and some
bacterium had begun to eat out everybody's eyes
so yellow pus spilled from the lower lids like sick tears

God was a bucket I spoke into, so to protest His absence
or cruel subtlety, I stopped speaking to Him. I ran away
from the land where I never heard His voice.

I hightailed it out.
Nobody sent after me for I was lazy and feckless and poor
at most orders, and I served an inescapable master:

In my head it sits
ugly and loud, hands on the controls
peering out my pie-slit eyeholes—speaking
the voice of my mother telling me to go
make a cardboard sign with a city on it,
stick your thumb out,
run, you little bitch . . .

V. Chronicles: Hell's Kitchen

Now I live on an island with two million souls
near the shell game and the sign with BUSINESS SUCKS

SALE and the barber hacking ice on the sidewalk
and a man squawking like a jungle toucan

crosses my path flapping his arms and charging
into the street so pedestrians part like water

arms flapping hard as if to leave this steaming earth
but gravity holds him among the rest of us

I come up late to my tenement with a key
in hand and in the doorway folded up

like an angular lawnchair a body
tilted head a snarl of tentacles

asleep with garbage bags layered on to keep off
rain so I must needs step over

his snoring form which rouses
to say in a rich baritone

worthy of Zeus, Excuse me

VI. Wisdom: The Voice of God

Ninety percent of what's wrong with you
   could be cured with a hot bath,
says God through the manhole covers,
   but you want magic, to win
the lottery you never bought a ticket for.
   (*Tenderly*, the monks chant,
embrace the suffering.) The voice never
   panders, offers no five-year plan,
no long-term solution, no edicts from a cloudy
   white beard hooked over ears.
It is small and fond and local. Don't look for
   your initials in the geese honking
overhead or to see through the glass even
   darkly. It says the most obvious shit,
i.e. Put down that gun, you need a sandwich.

VII. Judges: Awe and Disorder

Don't doubt for one blip every citizen of this place is an outlaw.
Just stand on a curb, each body strains against its leash,
no intention of not walking when the red, pixelated hand
lights up like a cop's. Even that humped-over old broad
shoves her silver walker into the oncoming bus's path
and dares it to flatten her. I'll bet way back
on the Emerald Isle when the landowner
Lord Suck-On-This rode up on his steed
instructing his henchmen to pull
a sod hut down on the children
as the smallest girl crawled out
to pelt the great rearing stallion
with moldy potatoes, and it's she now bent
shoves the walker with the force
of her years here.

And that mere slip of a man slim as a brushstroke
trying to sleep in that doorway—when Mao's henchmen
rushed toward his mother, who set out across the frost field
with him strapped to her back, and the dry stalks

crackling under her stride like glass
smashed on the tyrant's photo.

We draw mustaches
on the Madonna and our musclemen sometimes don drag.
We're the naysayers, the risk-takers. I came here cowed
and heartbroke. The first rat I saw scramble across my path
heard a shriek. Now, the vermin catch my boot sole.
Roaches flee from my light switch.
Bring us your fuse lighters, your bomb wirers.
Ply our teeth from our mouths we'll scream bloody
curses against your progeny.

VIII. Obadiah: A Perfect Mess

I read somewhere
that if pedestrians didn't break traffic laws to cross
Times Square whenever and by whatever means possible,
the whole city would grind to a halt.
Cars would back up to Rhode Island,
an epic gridlock not even a cat
could thread through. It's not law but the sprawl
of our separate wills that keeps us all flowing. Today I loved
the unprecedented gall
of the piano movers, shoving a roped-up baby grand
up Ninth Avenue before a thunderstorm.
They were a grim and hefty pair, cynical
as any day laborers. They knew what was coming,
the instrument white lacquered, the sky bulging black
as a bad water balloon and in one pinprick instant
it burst. A downpour like a firehose.
For a few heartbeats, the whole city stalled,
pauses, a heart thump, then it all went staccato.
And it was my pleasure to witness a not

insignificant miracle: in one instant every black
umbrella in Hell's Kitchen opened on cue, everyone
still moving. It was a scene from an unwritten opera,
the sails of some vast armada.
And four old ladies interrupted their own slow progress
to accompany the piano movers,
each holding what might have once been
a lace parasol over the grunting men. I passed next
the crowd of pastel ballerinas huddled
under the corner awning,
in line for an open call—stork-limbed, ankles
zigzagged with ribbon, a few passing a lit cigarette
around. The city feeds on beauty, starves
for it, breeds it. Coming home after midnight,
to my deserted block with its famously high
subway-rat count, I heard a tenor exhale pure
longing down the brick canyons, the steaming moon
opened its mouth to guzzle from on high . . .

IX. Ecclesiastes: Amok Run

Who could deny that one in twenty thousand would as soon
Run among you wheeling an axe. I myself confined

In a subway car befumed by the farts of strangers do wish them
Heartily dead, which I text my son who texts back,

You are so not a shepherd. My America has Glocks in it.
I growl most days over the bones of whatever I've paid for.

Mine own neighbor in his slot across the hall
From my slot used to strike me as a bachelor eccentric—

Collecting opera scripts and papers stacked floor to ceiling
Like kindling. Then I came in at three a.m., up

The old tenement stairs to find him squiring a street boy
Perhaps fourteen out his apartment door. Furtive, this man

Scuttling past like a scorpion, the boy moving as if drugged
Holding the banister. He looked Native American

And had a hickey on his pencil neck and black scars
Inside his arms from recent needles.

How long that night I stared at my spackled ceiling
Till at dawn I knocked on said neighbor's door

To declare: We won't have any more
Drugged-up boys in here now, will we?

X. Psalms: Carnegie Hall Rush Seats

Whatever else the orchestra says,
the cello insists, You're dying.
It speaks from the core

of the tree's hacked-out heart,
shaped and smoothed like a woman.
Be glad you are not hard wood

yourself and can hear it.
Every day the cello is taken
into someone's arms, taken between

spread legs and lured into
its shivering. The arm saws and
saws and all the sacred cries of saints

and demons issue from the carved cleft holes.
Like all of us, it aches, sending up moans
from the pit we balance on the edge of.

XI. Hey Jude: Prophetic Interlude by the Ghost of Walt Whitman

Out of the ether I have come to speak to you
Off the right-angled sidewalks of this city,
A place whose food carts scorch the flesh

Of many slaughtered lambs.
I am a scout sent to label what's vanishing, to capture in bell jar
The whiff of lime leaves and coconut milk from Go-Go Curry

Where the prayer rugs unroll five times per day so men
Can bow to the eternal while huffing taxis double-park outside
Unmolested by pumpkin-orange parking tickets

And the Now Baking sign never stops flashing. There are buns
In many ovens, and I record their rise and the passing
Of minor saints: the woman whose lavender hair

Is the shade of faded irises as she conducts a discourse with
The Invisible: finger raised in a pose that evokes Confucius
or Socrates. I chronicle the industry of the Garment District

Where a giant speaking some Slavic language into his headset
Shoulders a box of rolled-up Chinese silks—gold butterflies,
Scarlet dragons, white chrysanthemums like fireworks

On emerald cloth. The rolls poke up like organ pipes.
The pedestrians this day are not maggots on meat,
But dancers who weave and heft their packages

To clear a path for each gliding profile.

XII. Malachi: Truckload of Nails

In the bright stutter of neon, the truck's driver
   feels the stock prices fluctuate
across his newly shaved face. His shirt is white linen.
   His mouth is now shaping the name
of Jehovah, who set us loose upon this hurtling earth.
   The truckload of nails is packed
to explode among the soft pink and black
   and beige bodies running
to and from their separate containers—many
   gnawed up inside, serpents
hatching in heads, while in one of the city's
   sewers oozing steam there's a device
wired to a cheap drugstore alarm, the scarlet digits
   counting down, and only the rats watching.

XIII. Hebrews: The Mogul

Some childhoods are so powerful
they drag on a man's soul like a magnet.

By day, he stands in boardrooms
silhouetted by the slide projector's beam.

Above twelve hanging neckties, a dozen faces
tip up at him like kids watching a cake carried out.

His laser light sweeps across a landscape.
It always lands in the spot

where the treasure can be dug for.
At sunset, they escort him to the limo.

Each man presses into his palm a card
with name embossed. They wave

from under the awning as snow falls.
Because it's Berlin, the consonants spoken

are sharp as barbed wire in his head
yet muffled by memory and snow.

The black car glitters inside with crystal,
amber spirits, VSOP. One sip, and his head

nods. The man's soul is sucked under time
as through a pneumatic tube.

He goes burrowing back and back
to another century when the mother figure

slips her wedding band under his tongue.
She ties a bundle to his back, her face wet

as the train doors seal her away forever.
Auf Wiedersehen . . . Then a long gauntlet

of gargoyles his stubby legs flee
across brown stalks in a frozen field.

He balls himself up all small in a haystack
as pitchforks jab, and every scream swallowed.

Later, he'll stand at the wall
of windows on the world, snapping the neck

on a water bottle as one might murder
a wounded bird. The tower he stands in

is flown at by two planes aimed at his unblinking,
the sky flawless blue when his line ends.

XIV. Lamentations: The More Deceived

(for George Saunders)

The jackhammer the man in the crosswalk wrestles with
He also leans on. It shimmies the cage holding his heart.
He wears royal blue tee over jelly belly, and his yellow helmet

Casts a gray veil over his face. The shaking moves up
Through my legs so the bone marrow shivers.
The air swims with swirling particles that make us ghosts.

At the crosswalk, the worker pauses to lift his face. We *see*
Each other: Hello, fellow sufferer! Many ways to become dust.
When the towers shed their flaming skins we'd first seen

Bodies falling from high windows like acrobats.
Those flights so brief, and Hell too endless to ponder.
It lasts and lasts. That's the point, repeating its evil

Self to the damned in detail.
Weeks after the attack, the masked firemen
In rubber boots melting from the heat wore asbestos gloves

Like oven mitts to labor in the pit.
Alongside George, I clung to the hurricane fence
Around the perimeter encased in stench of burnt rubber.

We couldn't stop
Watching before everyone was saved,
Though it was a form of porn, of course.

The worst wasn't when firemen found
A bit of human matter — finger or tooth —
And it was placed on its own stretcher (so small!)

And some signal was given and all work came to a halt,
And men cupped their helmets over their heaving
Chests. The worst wasn't even the work starting back up

And men sliding their helmets back on and bending down
To rubble again as the stretcher with human matter
Snaked across the smoking pile to some tents —

The worst was looking into George's round glasses
At his dark blue and brimming eyes
As he said we were enjoined

By that smoking scene to live fully awake
Every instant after, for only presence
Could honor the lost, and yet neither of us was capable of it —

Not even for two minutes however much fasting and prayer,
For that big slutty whore of a city was beckoning,
And we wanted pizza and hand sanitizer, and had to hit

A fundraiser and, ergo, must shower the stench off ourselves.
And to escape the smoke, which we feared was scorching
Our otherwise pristine lungs, we walked down over rocks

By the water to find the fence where kids of the dead had wired
With baling wire stuffed bears and dolls with stiff arms
Outstretched for fucking ever and those last notes

Laminated and drawn in listing block print
By the small and weak and mostly illiterate.
Blue crayon tear, x eyes, frown face, prayer hands.

XV. Kings: The Obscenity Prayer

Our Falter, whose art is Heavy,
Halloween be thy name.
Your kingdom's numb
your children dumb on earth
moldy bread unleavened.
Give us this day our
wayward dead.
And empower our asses
that they destroy those
who ass against us.
And speed us not
into wimp nation
nor bequiver us
with needles, for thine
is the flimflam and the sour,
and the same soul-
sucking story in leather
for never and ever.
Ah: gin.

XVI. Marks and Johns: The Blessed Mother Complains to the Lord Her God about the Abundance of Brokenness She Receives

Today I heard a rich and hungry boy verbatim quote
all last night's infomercials — an anorectic son
who bought with Daddy's Amex black card
the Bowflex machine and Abdomenizer,
plus a steak knife that doth slice
the inner skin of his starving arms.
Poor broken child of Eve myself,
to me, the flightless fly,
the listing, blistered, scalded.
I am the rod to their lightning.
Mine is the earhole their stories pierce.
At my altar the blouse is torn open
and the buttons sailed across
the incensed air space of the nave,
that I may witness the mastectomy scars
crisscrossed like barbed wire, like bandoliers.

To me, the mother carries the ash contents
of the long-ago incinerated girl.
She begs me for comfort since my own son
was worse tortured. Justice,
they wail for — mercy?
Each prostrate body I hold my arms out for
is a cross my son is nailed to.

XVII. The Like Button

Back in the before time
those days of amber
desire was an inner
and often ugly thing.
And if we wanted,
my brothers and hungry
sisters, we were oft flung
far from each other. Think
tin-cans-and-string far,
plum-colored-smoke-signal
far. No web wove the pinpoints
of ourselves into a map. No
upward thumb could be pressed
to say yes or its detractor: no.
Soon, we may each evolve
a glow button maybe mid brow,
so as we pass each other we can vote
praise or scorn to light up yay
or nay on a passing stranger's face
a thumb. At first the young celebs

with asses you can serve drinks off
will rack up zillions of votes
till we tire of such bodacious butts,
and then the smart, the brave,
the strong will take their turns,
but what if we start to like,
say, the stout, the schlubby
neighbor raking leaves or that
subway sleeper who's woven
yellow crime scene tape into
a jock strap—Police Line: Do
Not Cross—till all the undeodorized,
the unloved all their lives, start to feel
their foreheads blip
and blip as it becomes hip
to love the oddest, the most
perilously lonely. Imagine
the forever dispossessed
transforming as they feel the thumb
of *yes* impress itself
into the very flesh.

XVIII. Petering: Recuperation from the Sunk Love Under the Aegis of Christ and Isaac Babel

If you spend all night reading Babel and wake on an island
    metropolis on your raft bed under a patent-leather sky
        with the stars pecked out, you may not sense
the presence of Christ, the Red Cavalry having hacked up
    all those Poles, the soldiers hugging each other
        with their hatchets. This morning, my ex-man
is a caved-in box of disposable razors to ship back.
    He wore a white Y on his baseball cap. Night
        was a waterfall down his face.
Marry me meant, *You're a life-support system*
    for a nice piece of ass; meant, *Rent*
        this space. Leaving the post office, I enter
the sidewalk's gauntlet of elbows. All around me,
    a locust buzz as from the book of Job. Yet I pray, I
        pray: Christ, my Lord, my savior,

and my good brother, sprinkle me
      with the blood of the lamb. Which words
          make manifest his buoyancy in me.
If the face of every random pedestrian is prayed for,
      then the toddler in its black pram
          gnawing a green apple can become baby Jesus.
And the swaggering guy in a do-rag idly tossing an orange
      into the crosswalk's air might feel heaven's winds
          suck it from his grasp as offering.
His gold teeth are a sunburst. When the scabby man
      festooned in purple rags shoulders an invisible rifle
          to shoot the do-rag dude, he pirouettes,
clutches his chest. Light applause follows
      his stagger to the curb. The assassin bows.
          These are my lords, my saviors, and my good brothers.
Plus the Jew Isaac Babel, who served the Red Calvary,
      yet died from a bullet his own comrade chambered.
          That small hole in his skull

is the spot on the map we sailed from.

XIX. Philemon:
Notes from the Underground

Tonight this subway car is permitted
to bear me in its belly through a black tunnel in rock.
  And in the evil of my pride, I get
to forget I am You-formed—needlework of hair
  stitched to my scalp growing outward,
stonework of bone, fret lines of tendon.
  In this dark vehicle, I sit unstrapped
among other similarly shaved animals.
  The long light above us is sick green,
the rivets holding our vehicle together are regular
  the way stars are not. They foretell
fuck all. I place my palms together, fingers unlit
  tapers invisibly burning for you.
Thirst is the truest knowledge of water.

XX. Revelation: The Messenger

It was anybody's son at the door
   in the dripping green slicker
      with the unsigned contract for selling my soul

to Holy-wood for a sack of gold
   the mere taxes on which would've once
      lit my greedy eyes with cartoon

dollar signs. The job was a trick I hoped
   to turn, having bankrupted myself on the dark,
      low-ceilinged box I lived in with plumbing from way

before Roosevelt. And as I looked for a pen
   I asked him in, and he asked to snapshot
      what he saw as my posh digs with battered camera

from a long lost pre-digital age. Cramming
   for his builder's exam, he was, the terms
      cornice and *chair rail* were enchanted spells

he was proud to master. And this
   new messenger job—which kept him weaving
      between cabs and buses on this

thundered day, to stand in wet helmet
   in my foyer—beat like hell his last
      hauling bags of tacos up the graffitied

halls of public housing. Better wage,
   better tips, nicer rooms to imagine
      he might hammer together once

he got certified. He rode off in a zigzag,
   dodging a bus that belched smoke.
      You won't believe his name was Jesus,

and I'd been weeks entreating the iron gray
   sky to see specifically Him. O Lord, last seen
      on battered mountain bike, green wings extended

behind in wind, come back, make me rich again.

Coda Toward the New New Covenant:
Death Sentence

(for Father Joseph Kane)

We lean close when the dying speak
though instinct says recoil from
the decaying form, but silence
radiates off them and blooms our loud
selves out, out, out of the way, and we long
to know what from each essential
self will exhale over us, and if we every
single one of us (it would only work
if we all agreed) listened to our own
deaths growing inside us geologically
slow inching forward as the skull
will someday edge through skin, then we would
each speak only the truest lines:
I've always loved you.

About the Author

MARY KARR's four books of poetry include *Sinners Welcome*, *Viper Rum*, *The Devil's Tour*, and *Abacus*. Her poetry secured her fellowships from the Guggenheim, the NEA, and the Bunting Institute at Radcliffe College. She's published three bestselling memoirs credited with kick-starting a renaissance in the form—*Lit*, *Cherry*, and *The Liars' Club*—as well as *The Art of Memoir*, which was also a *New York Times* bestseller. Her Syracuse graduation speech, published as *Now Go Out There*, lit up the Twittersphere. Her Americana song collaboration with country hunk Rodney Crowell, *Kin*, reached number one on the charts and was a Grammy finalist. Her book on aging, *Just You Wait*, is in progress.

Karr is the Peck Professor of Literature at Syracuse University and commutes there from New York City, where she is grandmother to a pit bull.

BOOKS BY MARY KARR

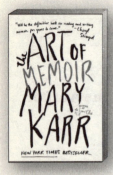

THE ART OF MEMOIR
Available in Hardcover, Paperback, and Ebook

Mary Karr offers a master class in the essential elements of great memoir—delivered with her signature wit, insight, and candor.

LIT
A Memoir
Available in Paperback, Ebook, and Large Print

Mary Karr's bestselling, unforgettable sequel to her beloved memoirs *The Liars' Club* and *Cherry*.

NOW GO OUT THERE
(and Get Curious)
Available in Hardcover and Ebook

A celebration of curiosity, compassion, and the surprising power of fear, based on Karr's 2015 commencement address at Syracuse University.

SINNERS WELCOME
Poems
Available in Paperback and Ebook

Mary Karr describes herself as a black-belt sinner, and *Sinners Welcome* traces her improbable journey from the inferno of a tormented childhood into a resolutely irreverent Catholicism.